If I Died, Would You Marry Again?

If I Died, Would You Marry Again?

AND OTHER BIG QUESTIONS

OF MARRIED LIFE

ANNA TOCHTER

Angus&Robertson
An imprint of HarperCollins*Publishers*

DEDICATION

To my husband with love –
I don't deserve you!

A.T.

Contents

The Handyman ◆ Boys' Night Out

The Green-Eyed Monster ◆ The Joy of Beauty

Truth or Dare ◆ It Must Have Shrunk

The Weaker Sex ◆ Where Are My Car Keys?

Do Not Disturb ◆ Domestic Duties

Deaf Wish ◆ Driving ◆ Never a Cross Word

Sex ◆ The Patter of Tiny Feet

 The Mother-in-Law

The Big Question ◆ The Even Bigger Question

Introduction

When I was young it seemed that married people were incredibly grown up. I now know this not to be the case. I have noticed an extraordinary similarity between the conversations between spouses and those we have with children.

As an experienced spouse much of my everyday conversation is *not* spent on weighty and life-shaping issues. It is spent repeating phrases such as 'Well, where did you leave your glasses last?' and 'No, it hasn't shrunk, I think you're putting on weight'. I'm particularly fond of 'No, I haven't moved your shoes' and 'Are these what you're looking for?'

I don't know how helpful my husband finds these daily exchanges, but I do know (from talking to other wives) how universal this banter is.

And the reason for this? *Men and women are different.*

While matters of sex, religion and politics may have drawn you together in the first place, these are *not* the issues that make or break a marriage. It is the ability to pick up the wet towels from the bathroom floor, remember where you saw the car keys and to keep your mouth shut during a crisis, that will keep the enterprise going.

This little book is a collection of my most favorite and recognizable his-and-her exchanges about the big questions of married life.
It's a mere part of the whole... reminisce, enjoy...

Anna Tochter

One year of joy, another of comfort,
and all the rest of content

17th Century English Proverb

Love & Marriage

From such innocent beginings...

Will you always love me?

◆

You'd never lie to me, would you?

I'll never leave you

◆

You don't want a big wedding, do you?

◆

How about we just elope?

◆

How many children do you want?

◆

Are you *sure* you want children?

What Day Is It Today?

In the tyranny of anniversaries, women have the advantage. They remember everything and for every moment in a relationship there is an anniversary...no wonder men 'forget'

Oh no, is it today?

◆

Has it really been that long?

◆

It seems like only yesterday

◆

I thought it was next month

◆

Didn't we agree that we wouldn't give each other presents?

Ah Yes, I Remember It Well...

Women remember certain things better than men...

Do you remember the time we went to Greece?

◆

That was the other wife

◆

Are you sure?

Oh You Shouldn't Have —

By and large women experience the joy of gift giving more than men. Most men go into a blind panic at the thought of having to buy presents, partly because it involves going shopping in shops and partly because they have no idea what the woman they live with actually wants.

I don't want anything

◆

Honestly darling

◆

Just something small

◆

Really darling, it's just lovely

Oh!

◆

What is it?

◆

Thanks, I know I needed a new iron

◆

This isn't my size/my color/my taste

◆

Did you choose this yourself, or did someone help you?

◆

Was it expensive?

◆

Did you keep the receipt?

Mothers' Day

But I thought you didn't believe
in that sort of thing

Types of Husbands

#1 The Mannequin

*I didn't marry one of these myself
but I have heard of those who have the nerve
to criticize how other people iron their shirts*

#2 The Raconteur

My wife has heard this story a million times

◆

My wife will correct me if I get it wrong

◆

Do you always have to spoil the punchline?

#3 The Born-Again Father

Just *who* is having this baby?...

We're having a natural birth

◆

We don't believe in drugs

◆

We're going to breastfeed

#4 The Chef

A man destroys the kitchen, tells you how much more creative he is than you, gives you rampant indigestion by demanding praise every second mouthful and then leaves you to clean up...

Don't you like it?

◆

I followed the recipe

◆

Why can't we have meals like this every night?

◆

Shall we have this again?

◆

When?

◆

Is this your favorite, or was last night's?

#5 The Employer

Did you manage to pick up the drycleaning?

◆

What do you mean you didn't have time?

◆

What do you *do* all day?

#6 The Agoraphobe

Oh no, we don't have to go out do we?

#7 The Selective Agoraphobe

You know I hate movies/Thai food/her husband

Wifely Advice #1

Don't you think you've had enough?

Wifely Advice #2

You're going to feel terrible tomorrow

Wifely Advice #3

I think it's time we went home

Nagging

You don't have to go on you know

◆

I heard you the first time

◆

But I *told* you

Wifely Surveillance

What was that look for?

◆

What did I say?

◆

How was I to know?

◆

Ow!

Bathroom Etiquette

*The key to a happy marriage is separate bathrooms.
Men regard bathrooms as a wet zone, splashing around like
sea lions, while women regard them as dry zones, believing
water should be confined to the designated areas.
And the incompatability doesn't end there...*

Who used my razor?

◆

Who left the top off the toothpaste?

There's no need to open a new soap,
there's plenty of the old one left

◆

Can't you *ever* pick up the wet towels?

◆

Towels will never dry folded like that

◆

Who took all the hot water?

◆

They're not *my* hairs in the basin

◆

You missed

◆

Why can't you put the seat down?

Household Management

There's nothing like a good spend,
but profligate or penny pinching,
each sex has an inclination towards
one or other theories of budgeting

#1 The Miracle of the Electric Light

Do we need every light in the house on?

◆

But there's no one in the room

◆

Did you see the size of the last electricity bill?

#2 The Miracle of the Electric Telephone

Why can't people call us?

◆

Do you have to be on the phone all the time?

◆

Is that long distance?

#3 The Miracle of the Gas/Fuel/Rates Bills

The miracle is that we can still afford to pay them

#4 Savings to Be Made in Sales

Economics 1

It's obvious that an item marked down
from $100 to $75 saves $25.
Do this four times and you have one item free
and you've saved $100!

Economics 2

When informing your spouse of a purchase,
always knock at least 25% off the price –
it makes you both feel better

Isn't That New?

A very amusing and well-loved game...

What, this old thing?

◆

I've had it for ages

◆

I bought it in a sale, it was a bargain

◆

I haven't got a thing to wear

Always marry a short woman,
her clothes will cost you less

Moroccan Proverb

The Handyman

Neither side is at its best here.
Men do and women criticize.
Tact is essential here, along with the Yellow Pages...

Will this take long?

◆

Will it make a mess?

◆

Do you think it's meant to look like that?

Are you sure you're following the instructions?

◆

There must be a piece missing

◆

I think that bit goes the other way

◆

No one will notice

◆

Aren't you finished yet?

◆

This color looks different in the daylight

◆

I've changed my mind

◆

Actually I think it looked better the way it was

◆

Just a bit to the left

◆

Maybe we should get a man in

◆

I think it's a job for a professional, now

Boys' Night Out

Her:

No of course I don't mind

❖

It'll be nice to have an evening on my own

Him:

I don't really want to go

◆

I'd rather stay in with you

◆

It'll be boring anyway

◆

It wasn't my idea

◆

It's just the usual guys

◆

I'll be home early

◆

I won't drink too much

◆

Honestly

The Green-Eyed Monster

Of course, petty little remarks about the Ex
are not worthy of us, however...

She's not wearing very well is she?

◆

Well I think she looks *much* older than 35

◆

Her children need a firm hand

She seems to have put on a lot of weight
since we last saw her

◆

No *wonder* he left her

The Joy of Beauty

The older you get the longer it takes to look natural.
It also costs more and takes more space in the bathroom

What is all this stuff *for?*

◆

Why does it take you so long to get ready?

◆

You never used to need all this stuff

It Must Have Shrunk

We have changed over the years,
there's invariably more of us —
and it's not in the same places

Do you think I've put on weight?

◆

Don't be ridiculous, it fitted last summer

◆

Did you put this in the dryer?

◆

Can you see any grey hairs?

◆

Do you think I'm going thin on top?

Would you say I had a double chin?

◆

What do you mean I've got hairs
growing out of my ears?

49

Truth or Dare

*If I were a man I'd ask for my lawyer to be present
before I answered any of these...*

Do you notice anything different about me?

◆

Are you sure I look all right in this?

◆

Do you think it makes me look fat?

◆

Does it look all right from the back?

◆

Do *I* look all right from the back?

What do you think of this dress?

◆

Do you think it's too young for me?

◆

Why haven't you said anything about my new haircut?

◆

Don't you like it?

◆

I can't go out looking like this

◆

Be honest, how old do you think I look?

◆

It's all right, you can tell me the truth

The Weaker Sex

Men seem to suffer from illness a great deal...

Feel my head, I'm burning up

◆

I think I'm coming down with something

◆

It must be a virus

◆

I've looked it up in the book

◆

I think it's a rare tropical disease

I've got this terrible pain

◆

My left arm is numb

◆

I think I'm having a heart attack

Where Are My Car Keys?

On a random sample of one, it appears that men need help finding everything once it is no longer in their physical grasp. This section could also be called "Have you seen..."

Who moved my car keys?

◆

I left them right here

◆

They must have been stolen/the children/dog ate them

◆

Where are my glasses/shoes/clothes/socks?

◆

Where have you put my book/newspaper/
remote control for the TV?

◆

It was here a minute ago

What's my jacket doing in the closet?

◆

Who hung this up?

◆

I wouldn't have put it there

Are **these** *what you're looking for?*

Do Not Disturb

Although your husband is free to interrupt you at any time, he must never be interrupted during any of the following vital pursuits...

Sport

◆

Sport on TV

◆

Thinking about sport

◆

Reading a newspaper

◆

Watching the news

Domestic Duties

What a minefield this is, and how much
praise the smallest task needs...

Oh darling, I would have done that

◆

While you're up can you...

◆

But I unload the dishwasher

◆

But I looked after the children so you could have
the free time to go to the supermarket

Deaf Wish

I'm sorry, I didn't hear you

Isn't that the phone?

Isn't that the doorbell?

I'm sorry, I didn't hear the kettle/
the children/the sirens

Driving

Ah, a book in itself...

How do you know it was a woman driver?

◆

He's yelling because you didn't indicate

◆

There was a parking space back there

◆

We've gone past it now

◆

I know I said left but I meant right

◆

It didn't say it was one way on the map

◆

How do I know which way is north?

What does that flashing light mean?

◆

I *told* you you were going too fast

◆

Are you alright to drive?

◆

Here, let me drive

Never a Cross Word

*Grown-up men and women are at their mature,
rational best in an argument (naturally this section
doesn't arise from personal experience)*

Don't take that attitude with me

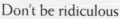

And what do you mean by that remark?

Are you trying to pick a fight?

Don't be ridiculous

Won't

Well, you started it

62

Typical, you always say that

◆

Why am I always in the wrong?

◆

Don't change the subject

◆

I can't believe you're saying this

◆

I can't believe I'm hearing this

◆

You're driving me insane

◆

I'm going out

◆

That's it – just walk away

◆

You always have to have the last word, don't you?

◆

Yes

Sex

You can have sex or you can have children
— you can't have both

How long has it been?

◆

Really! That long?

The Patter of Tiny Feet

*Left to their own devices, most men wouldn't
(or couldn't) initiate the issue of 'now we are three'*

Isn't it nice just the two of us?

◆

Why would we want to spoil it?

◆

How *can* you be pregnant?

◆

I think I have to sit down

Do you think the baby looks like me?

◆

Isn't it nice just the three of us

The Mother-in-Law

You tell her, she's *your* mother

The Big Question

If I died, would you marry again?

The Even Bigger Question

Think carefully before you answer this one

Who?

The Last Word

Marriage makes two one, but which one?

Anon

An Angus&Robertson Publication

Angus&Robertson, an imprint of HarperCollins Publishers
25 Ryde Road, Pymble, Sydney NSW 2073, Australia
31 View Road, Glenfield, Auckland 10, New Zealand
77-85 Fulham Palace Road, London W6 8JB, United Kingdom
10 East 53rd Street, New York NY 10022, USA

First published in Australia in 1994

National Library of Australia
Cataloguing-in-Publication data:
Tochter, Anna
If I died, would you marry again?: and other big questions of married life.

ISBN 0 207 18523 9

1. Marriage - Humor. Marriage - Quotations, maxims, etc.
3. Australian wit and humor. I. Title.

A828.302

Designed by Clare Forte
Printed in Hong Kong

9 8 7 6 5 4 3 2 1
97 96 95 94